T0158692

All the Verbs
for Knowing

Poems

GEORGE PERREAULT

Rainshadow Editions
The Black Rock Press
2006

ISBN 13: 978-1-891033-34-6

The Black Rock Press
University of Nevada, Reno Reno, NV 89557-0044
www.blackrockpress.org
Printed in the United States of America

Cover Image by Steve Laudermilch

Poems in this collection have previously appeared in the follow-
ing journals and anthologies: *Coastal Plains Poetry, Gruene Street,
High Country News, Journal of Curriculum Theorizing, Kalliope,
Message from the Heart, Multicultural Education, Nature's Advocate,
Northwest Review, Prayers of the Universe, Rocky Mountain Review,
Shenandoah,* and *The New Verse News.*

The title for the first section is taken from the closing lines of Pablo
Neruda's "Juegas Todos los Dias ...", which translates to, "I want to
do to you what spring does with the cherry tree."

for the lost

CONTENTS

Tongues

TONGUES

Early, moist, and The People risen
like a herd before me,
dark water solid as snake
and their speech one long word.

They have four verbs for knowing:
by the senses, by hearsay, by logic
and by intention, which is how
anything comes to happen.

I've learned enough to say
each deer is a prayer to Deer,
and each child a robe
to be worn by the tribe.

I have to leave before the rains:
in the next village I might find
that language where everything is
potential, even our own names.

by the senses ...

QUE LA PRIMAVERA HACE

IT'S NOT *AS IF*

It's not *as if* sometimes you're sixteen again:
this afternoon's really the first a man's
unbuttoned you, lifted, bent and kissed: here,
surrounded by blackberries
and zinnias.

And when you touch me back, it's not *like*
a wave sweeping the tidal pool: everything does
swell with power and with nourishment
and everything
is something else.

Love's no mere acquaintance:
our hands and lungs invent a language
in the voices of whose animals we
cry out the long translation
of each other's stubborn tongue.

You are that pear in the long autumn grass,
and when you rise from a bath warm and wet
my clothes are a trail of scraps in the folktale forest
and everything,
everything is metaphor.

SEEING SOMEONE

The planet tilts till new plants surge and
spill out into the air; young girls unveil their
whitest skin and we crane our necks toward light.

But when spring explodes upon us over and over,
driving the green stake deep into the heart,
how often we practice averting our eyes,

how often refuse to shake habituation,
to accept the embrace and involvement
with seeing that happens everywhere – even here,

in what looks like any airport lobby
full of harsh fluorescent glance and the
miasma of departure – look again,

at how we are wading toward each other,
this woman and I, the unschooled fishes
dancing among our legs, the red sun

sitting down in the clouds like a giant egg.
After however many days it was, we are
seeing each other now, and look:

the air itself a mirror of the heart, the breeze,
ripe with almonds, how it stirs with the wings
of ten thousand butterflies.

LISTENING TO HER

I speak so she might speak again and
her voice sets forth in fits and starts
pauses unanticipated and tumbles in
upon the ear, skipping from thought to
thought, breathless and throaty,
itself a living being – this yearling doe
who steps into the clearing, into a light
tremulous with desire, the slow flex
of her haunch as the liquid eye
mirrors surprise, curiosity, caution
passion regret acceptance
over and over: this puzzlement:
this endless delight and in-
evitable surrender.

DANCING NAKED ON THE MESA

It's spring and I'm climbing again
rising through piñon and alligator juniper
into the lives of birds and the open face of the sky,
shirt thrown back, pants, everything down to skin
flung to music, to the guttural urge
for a chant older than language, older
even than names – this raven croak, this head-back cry
I aim wherever you could be hiding,
every sandstone swell or shadow, every
delicate hint wet and green, and I'm dancing,
dancing to the darkhaired friend, to the wing drum,
dancing with a feathered strut and flutter and the long shriek
of mated falcons as they plunge toward earth and barely slide apart
into this dance, this naked hot and dusty dance, this
always and forever ache I ache for you.

PONIES

We ride like that little chestnut high on a butte
looking out over the Yellowstone,
the way she turns now and the muscles
twitch under her tight skin.

We ride like the rock-bound western river,
its quick colors and sudden pools
needled with trout, the shrill bugle
of elk in the cottonwood.

And we ride like autumn birds, the
rolling shadow on the fields,
the swoop and swirl here and
gone and back again, while we both

shake out our hair, gather
and thrust, gallop side by side
across that lavish range
until, finally

deep in the dark of the barn
the firefly pulse, neck on neck,
we can slide and ease
into almost separate thought.

SOME OF HER PARTS

I love her hair, the way it swings
against her cheek when she turns to smile,
how it shields our faces when she leans to me,
and when I take both hands and pile it high
no one has been wealthier than this.

I love the way her lower lip feeds into my teeth and how
the gentlest tug raises the primitive moan and her tongue
slips deep over mine, and when she draws my finger
down into her mouth and looks me full,
every half-truth peels to barest need.

I love how the ridge of her ear curves like a stem
to the succulent lobe and the way her long neck
offers itself up and back, and I drink
at the little pool where her bones are
hollowed sandstone in the shadow of a cliff.

And I love the exclamation of her breasts, the nipples
like children skipping in the surf, the ebb and swell of her
and the long scar of her birthing, how she bridges
like a wrestler, her loins like an altar, the pressure
of her thighs and her wild fragile hands.

I love her strong feet dancing the dark room
and the bright path she leads me, and how we lie down
out of the wind, against rocks washed with golden leaves
to practice the primordial numbers and wrap together,
summed and whole.

I DREAMED WE MERGED AND MOVED

where the fenceposts flower and the women
speak like Fiona Ritchey. I dreamed of the
warm evenings old men laughed on the green
and no one went home till he wanted. And I
dreamed we were wrapped alone in a hay loft
with rain on the tin and the long afternoon ahead,

and that you were walking on the shore of a lake,
late summer trees, silver pebbles beneath your feet,
downpour plastering your shirt, matting your thick hair, and
the way you stared at me, breathing hard and shallow. I dreamed
that we were eight, hiding behind the bridal wreath at the end
of the playground, and we stopped and smiled, each at the other.

And I dreamed this dream we're winding through canyons,
boulders, thin ribbons of sky, that every now and then
we blunder together, and maybe we're old friends, and
maybe later we'll yelp louder than coyotes, maybe
we'll merge and move where even the fenceposts
open their hands on the day.

CHATOYANCY

The walls now
a shade of green
hard pressed to say: like your eyes
at shimmer time

maybe westward off Plumas
geese straggle-gliding to the
flicker of Stevie Nicks:
stay with me, stay

and so maybe the drapes
really should dance the nubby breeze
joyous as your breasts' back and forth
under the evening gauze

maybe set it all aside and
let the river flow
down into sing then serene
where all the words are but one.

OH

an extra dark choco-
late: the slow
roll of it:

     loam and tendril
morning grass tiled with wet leaves
grapes heavy in the gray light

the rivered flavor coiled
roof and tongue and then
gone:

     a kingfisher
the air full of whisper
and me thinking about you

THERE IS NO NEED FOR THIS

the rainbow, the hawk,
alfalfa flush against basalt,
water silver in the reeds and all
these shades of green.

There is no need for the
sinuous contours of fields
or the crystal dazzle
of an ordinary road.

Why is the skin of this world so
enticing, when we could roll
and rut blind as moles,
dumber than worms?

What does it serve, nectar and blossom,
when we're slaves of hunger anyway,
when music plays upon us so, lifts
our feet and flings our hands about?

And why must a trace of herbal soap
drag back exact angles of your thighs,
the wetness of your hair, the secret
taste of you?

There is no need for this, no need,
nor can my heart withstand it –
the frontal assault on my senses
and the storm of memory too.

WATER STRIDERS

My eye traced a face on a face in the paper:
a girl I once knew, younger than you'd think –
a few hours on blackberry roads, a few mornings
in an iron framed bed, and even, years later

entranced in the sheen of a city,
the scent of her rich dark hair –
I knew I was in trouble, she laughed,
as soon as I looked at you.

There is a color along the edge of the brook
the exact brown of her eyes, just over the sandbar,
out where leaves gather thick and old and the light
slants down and dances on water striders –

their shadowed feet the tense black notes
on which we skim, vibrating with memory –
the sun opening its mouth, her skin
alive, alive in my skittering hand.

COMING & GOING

Though it's a rare surprise, still she
likes to hear my yes and tells me then
to hold us still and let her come again.
There are things, of course, we may not speak –
whose thighs engaged us now, whose
heights and depths considered–but speaking itself,
that other intercourse, catches my thought:
how different in French – *je va, je va* – I go.

How absolutely male that seems, how
adventurous, like going away for the summer
or going off like fireworks, the smoke
drifting east up the river, this girl I'm going with
going down on me – first we go to town
and then we go to pieces, you know how
that story goes: how death eventually goes and spoils
everything, how in the end we all go
back where we came from.

But where are we when we come?
Coming to some conclusion or coming perhaps
even to perfection – the answer came to me
in a dream: we're coming to our senses, my ears
pounding as the artillery comes into action,
as she churns till the butter comes,
until the sob comes up in her throat,
until we come to see each other as this
coming home, this coming back to the small
harbor with that lighthouse flashing
how I trust and trust and trust in you.

SONG IN THE KEY OF SPRING

sometimes in my yard,
sheltered in salt cedar, a flock
of yellow-headed
blackbirds will
pause and
catch their breath

and again it's that southern street
where the saxophone
solos
just for grateful lovers
graced like bourbon
in a glass of sunlit jazz

while dark the sweetwet April river
laps against the shore – the
bonfire of your legs –
that moonspun fluttery cave
everything's nothing but
swirl

RE: INCARNATION

this whole season of travels:
lobbies and shuttles
ballparks, barbecues
winding the sides
of slouched volcanoes
heat rising in
slow salted spirals
old groves so thick
they own the air itself
everywhere my eyes
among the treasured museums
and throbbing taverns
under the lindens
seeping in the night
the ocean's hiss and lick and
everywhere women wear jeans –
and everywhere the endlessly varied
cotton blue handclasp constricts
my throat, tongue curled
dry and black while
the estuarian prayer eels
under and explodes straight
from my heart o lord
sweet lord next time I'm back
next time
sweet lord
just let me be denim

by hearsay ...

LISTENING TO THE ELDERS

GYPSIES

Years ago it was, they'd rein
the cluttered wagons and ask for water:
some special tree, my father thought,
must be marked along the road.

There are signs all around us
we can't read. And there are
things we don't understand how
we know: that ragged man's

penniless but not destitute, that he
cares for this woman who laughs
and staggers and rages at demons
as we wait for the light to change.

It's downhill, he promises, all the way
to the river, and we'll lie tonight
in green murmur, watch willows
sign the cool well of the moon.

SHE TELLS ME

tomatoes technically are fruit,
and like so many they ripen
not by light, but by heat.

       She tells me
on the canoe trip was a long whistling no one else caught
but I learned of a massacre in the old books, tribe
against tribe, and how even now one might hear
the women wail their dead,
clean as a knife.

       She tells me
remember that girl in the camisole? – the lungs
yanked out of your body driven to the knees
your face in a paper bag to gasp and
giggle how stupid while the railroad
spike rips through your head
and she tumbles this is better than flowers.

THE WORDS WE USE

She had a story, I tell Rattler,
of the wind breathing thank you
and how she knew it was her grandmother
deep in the clean grave, a cool late August morning
high on the empty plains. What's the word, I asked him,
your people use for that?

I'm not sure, he said; there's a few she might've used.
There's one for blessing, the open hand.
And there's one for butterfly, how it brushes away
spaces between you, and your heart smiles.
The others, they're pictures too –
it's not like English.

And I saw great aunt Mamie,
the year my father braved the blizzard
to bring her home for Christmas dinner,
mother clucking and walking circles, how foolish it was
and her sister echoing and finishing sentences
the way family sometimes do.

But my father went and later took her back,
the only car on the road all afternoon,
mother's eyes cold as the storm,
and this her aunt, not his,
the one that put the girls through teachers college
after grandpa Hiland died.

My father told me later how Mamie clutched his arm
in both hands, tighter than he thought she could
saying, thank you, thank you, the way an eagle
shows its gratitude for trout, the way I split
tamarack and red cedar, cry
night fire sweet woman love.

I DO, SHE SAID

some of my best writing in airports
surrounded by garbled instruction
and a self-important crowd: badges
and buckles, team jackets: Philadelphia
fighters on their way to crash in Poland,
my lover's sputter at the sidebars,
who caught or missed that flight

when everything is random,
we could just fly apart:
who knows what's to come:
a summer sailing,
that open doorway,
my body's banner
given to another's hands.

Here among the disconnected,
the only place some regularly read,
I struggle with intractable language,
how to say *my child dead of cancer:*
not just clouds, but
clouds on the face of a lake,
and the wind rising.

THE DEATH OF DEER

For Richard Nelson

We are all involved, he writes to us,
whether we walk with careful prayer
or stumble in a drunken slog,
whether we cheer the end of those
who would chew our orchards bare
or eat nothing but leaf and grain,
we are all involved with the death of deer.

And we are all involved with the death of fish
whether we still seek that startled tug
or tend cultured roots which spin
poisoned filaments into the lungs of the sea
or float the market whispering halibut,
albacore under the murderous light:
we are all involved with the death of fish.

And we are all involved with the daily news:
with the homeless, the Haitians, and the suicides,
with fires in Sarajevo and Los Angeles,
with bloated bellies in Somalia and Sudan,
with women beaten up and down our streets
and with the greed and lust of our secret dreams
which puddle and shimmer upon the floor.

We are inextricably involved in everything:
the exhalation of forests and Bhopal's lethal breath;
we are brother to tiger and sister to shark
and though we might wish our hands were clean,
we are built of blood and dirt and the music
anything sings when it circles its mouth to feed:
succored by wolves, we lift our muzzle to deer.

SOUTHERN CUSTOMS

Some places they
cut parts out of people and
toss them into the street.

Some places they
hand you
the knife.

THIS POEM

is about eating a sandwich and watching
a 51 Pontiac slide through the parking lot
while a B-52 lumbers back to base
as the technician upgrades my memory
and my brother lies dying 2500 miles away.

This poem is about his wife canceling
the CAT scan: if it hurts that much to be moved,
and there's nothing we don't already know . . .
most of the time he can't recognize her
and maybe it's better that way.

This poem is about my sister saying how
when he was home he thought the living room
was a funeral parlor and he couldn't understand
why his children weren't there,
you'd have thought they'd say goodbye.

This poem is about my brother who thinks
there's a dead dog in the room, and no one
does anything except ask out loud:
What is madness? What is metaphor?
What is this awful poem we speak?

NAMING THE INDIANS—
CROW AGENCY, 1897

I believe there are simple rules in this matter.
A surname in their vernacular may be kept, if short,
or a syllable or two of a long one, if melodious
and inoffensive, may be retained for a family name.

Always consider, however, how easily one may
go astray when wrestling with their Indian tongues.
Among the Apaches a policeman brought in a boy
and when the superintendent inquired of his name

"Des-to-dah," said the federal and rode away. And so
with the addition of a pleasingly Christian first name
the boy became "Matthew Destodah" though the last
was merely an Indian word for "I don't know."

Of course, some other names are ridiculous
and should never be perpetuated – Kills-the-one-
with the-blue-mark-in-the-center-of-the-chin.
This is uncouth, un-American, uncivilized.

And further, in their curious custom,
these names will vary from friends to enemies,
so the one that you might call Six-bears
in the other village will be Afraid-of-his-horse.

Even worse, as an Indian child grows, he may commit,
from time to time, acts engendering further names. If
Wide-smile is frightened and dashes screaming home
he will be called Runs-from-a-fox.

Then as a young man he may ride his horse
out among the enemy and be called Charges-
through-the-camp, or should he slay someone
in battle, Kills-the-one-with-the-big-knee.

So we see Indian names are nothing, a delusion
and a snare, and the practice of converting them
into English appears most unwise. Thus, it is
inevitably better to grant them English names –
choose a proper first name, of course, and then obtain,
from their own tongue, the family name by
an arbitrary shortening which renders a sound
at once euphonious and obscure.

AT THE HERTFORD ASSIZES, 1622

You would I not tarry
but say now as so lightly then:
There, in a wind of snowbirds,
walked a spotted cat
with the face of Jane Wenham.

Words for your words
but I wish you heard of others:
Just last month in St. Blais
a stray dog hanged
for eating meat on Friday.

And next Sabbath morn
our hooded men shall lay
careful changeling fires
to darken the fallow air
with the bones of Jane Wenham.

EARLY MORNING ON WASSERGASS

easing into the eventual light, the gradual
indifference of frogs, Len's old white cat
creaky as me

as I think how maybe there is in Russian
one precise word for any relative –
my brother's wife's sister –

and some system for delineating relations where
kinship counts more than that this woman's
just moved to my old hometown

across from my first girlfriend's where it's always
summer, the night porch,
Janice, alone

my fingers like a science project all step by step
care and hope and never a trace
of objectivity

and maybe in Russian or probably German,
that moon-thick tongue, there's a term
for what I still chase

drink after drink on the night pier
that sound beyond division
beyond partition

the one word that means everything –
cat pond mist, the delicious light-
headed ooze and echo

beyond the distant thrum and plosh
while the day slides up like Janice
cerulean, white, and ready

COLD COMFORT

My mother was of a tribe
in which elders crawl into the wilderness
to die.

She took the dark passage in winter
while the night filled with her singing
the virtues of ice.

SOMETIMES

Where do we pass,
shadow to shade and
enter welcoming?

Maybe times we give it up,
the strained culmination of our days,
just drop it on shore and wade out deep.

I've tried that now and then and
seen you there besides,
which is only natural

when death slides
his bad shit
deep into our veins.

But again sometimes
maybe high above the ocean
the moon swells a level pathway

and we waltz the dark waltz
along the bronzed archipelago
of our breath.

Sometimes we pass that way,
shadow to shade – please god
we pass that way

THANKFULNESS

When I hear of Jesus, I think *man* first,
maybe a man walking alone by the sea.
It's night, and he's tired and
I wouldn't say sad exactly
but *melancholy*,
maybe thinking, not of those few who have
opened their eyes and see the divine everywhere,
even in you and me,
but he was thinking instead of people like me
(and maybe even like you),
people who do not always look on a sister's face and say
"Belovéd gift of God,"
not always,
not nearly enough,
but sometimes, praise God, sometimes
we do, even me
as when asked for a word of thankfulness
for those we see every day

I thought at once of your face,
the way your smile opens like Raven's wing
and changes everything.
I thought how
any day I needed
I could walk up to you
and put my heart in your hands
and you would hold it
like a precious thing.
And I thought how each of us could say that of someone,
maybe of more than one, and this
in a world where children shoot other children
for standing on their shadows.

I thought of how the last time I was
crazy in love
she was everywhere in the crowd –
in the hustlers, the winos, even the businessmen,
some gesture or turn of phrase –
that tired housewife: her hair
my lover's hair.

So maybe we make it too hard,
this dream of perfect community.
I say
love the one.
Love the one neighbor well.
Look out over the railroad tracks
where the wasted and broken souls
shuffle, always alone, through the snow,
and then come home to the face of your friend,
to those whose deepest wish is for you to be, at last,
nothing but yourself,
and give thanks, one friend at a time,
one neighbor at a time
while we grow,
flower by flower,
into the garden of God.

VESPERS

Tonight in Mission Park, the homeless offer up
their battered tale: "That kingfisher by the river,
he's bigger than an eagle"

and I speak as I've learned to the gentle mad,
those voices tangential to mine,
a promise to be careful.

"Oh, there's no need to worry," they say, "not you –
he's just carrying off the dead."
And I remember that bird:

One night on the plains the seven-foot hawk
knocked upon my dreams, took me
carefully into his claws

and lifted with long, sinuous strokes, above
sectioned fields, wheat and cattle and
little tree-wrapped towns,

above the abstract demarcations that scarify our days,
above pain and hunger and the stale crust of habit,
above the black edge of life itself.

And when he was done with me, set down
and draped his wing across my shoulder
and showed me to the door.

Still, there are days, even whole weeks which pass
and I forget to think of him, that great bird
of mercy.

But tonight, from this place beside the river, please
may he hear, better than an owl, the cooling
embers of my brother's brain;

may he hear the caught breath of his wife and children
held until their sides ache
even in their sleep.

Come down, great bird, kingfisher or hawk, come down
to the dark side of the planet and
lift my brother clean.

by logic ...

THIS, THEN THAT

COMING BACK FROM OKANOGAN

You cross the river east south east and note
how volcanoes and irrigation define the West
and that maybe taking separate cars is not
like anything else: how you have to calculate
ahead and behind and the traffic decides
not just for you but for the one who trails,
with a pickup between, through towns where
they play eight-man football and at least half
the cheerleaders are virgins but each of their
breasts is its own little animal, and you
pay more attention to every curve, whether
she's keeping pace and when you have to ease
a while and how, when snow begins to spit
as you twist down the Coulee, it asks that you
weigh everything twice: the dusk, the impending
miles, the trucks slow and heavy with hay:
it's not like conversation, or marriage, or even
like making love; it is what it only is:
a late afternoon in mid-October, driving back
from Okanogan through the weathered hush.

POKER NIGHT AT MOUNT SPOKANE

The autumn geese rise soft above the land,
and their wild cries hush the table where
we deal the cards which will become our hand.

Our cigars smolder down to their gaudy bands
as curving smoke carves a body in the air
like autumn geese rising soft above the land.

By brunt of silence we sometimes are unmanned,
or the face of time's wreckage, disease and war:
we hold those cards which have become our hand;

but whisky rubs the glass like water on the sand
of the morning marsh we hunted without care
for autumn geese which rise soft above the land,

and now beyond our aim, survivors of their clan,
wholly living birds, southward take the dare
while we hold the cards which have become our hand.

We're dealt some days on which to put our brand,
to drink the spirits and breathe them into prayer,
to play the cards which have to be our hand
then, like autumn geese, rise soft above the land.

LEARNING TO DRIVE

There's always a sense of audience,
someone to remark any stutter as you
begin to master the shift, that
delicate little dance, hands and feet
aimed at an oily click, or perhaps
a brassy double-clutch to swing
the flatbed into the yard loaded with bales.

Shifting's about that effortless merge,
someone else breathing *of course,*
whereas steering is an act
redolent of purpose. It is more
consonant with might than with
might have been. From the first
it is Nietzsche, not Lao Tzu.

But every farm road has some corners
where the dirt is worn in ways
it knows you want to go.
You are in love with this truck.
You close your eyes and bring it
into third. You lift your hands
and push the pedal down.

GOING HOME FROM THE CLINIC

The elevator rises from the wing
where we strip their senses clean:
the girl for whom snow falls
like endless shattered glass,
the men who see mirrors shiver
like girls in naked chain.

Along the walk outside, every willow's
triggered with light, thought after thought
swimming the coral brain. Yesterday
the feral child fled to the mesa,
her hands slapping at language, her hair
trailing like female rain.

Today was Aaron, in whose ears the soil
wars root over root while lichen gnaw
the granite bones. The rocks,
I ask, are even the rocks alive?
Not all, he thinks, though some of them
surely are.

And some nights the river smells
of white linen, and the streets throb
like the harbor of your heart.
But in the places my people live,
night bears down with the full
dumb weight of the stars.

CAPTURED

In the wide-angled black and white a
girl turns over her left shoulder where
the steps leave the plaza and regards the
boy who leaps up and clicks his heels,
the hands behind his back loaded with roses,
and immediately I'm back in the doorway

as you walk in from the balcony
after your husband's foolish mime and
the hidden treat he thought was sweetened
by this latest trick while you waited among us
with your usual unexpressed anger.
 "Women," he shrugged, and turned away.

How easy to think I could have
sat down beside you then, how easily said
"When you get tired of this shit
just let me know" and everything
would have been different – but it's
only now we are who we are,

only now we can understand
everyone's watching from some doorway
most of the time, and what we need to do,
finally, is walk out onto the empty plaza and
let that thing which yearns to leap up
leap up and click its salty heels.

WOLVES IN THE WALLPAPER

an angle of light or the lengthening
year and wolves in the wallpaper
take our measure

the golden wolf of the groin who
does you fast like
some smash and grab thug:
three bites and a lick and his
callow eyes never blink

the green wolf of the intestines:
his casual patience, his
democracy:
how he ranges before you
food and drink, flesh and spirit,
whatever slivered desire
calcifies or blossoms
to eat you inside out

the blue wolf of the chest
hunched on the tundra gnawing
the weathered bone of your breath:
a scrap of marrow,
murmured rumors of your heart
taking
taking

the red wolf of the face,
the nameless skin dangling your
shredded jaw, the tongue's
slow fish flop
the bubbled wind, the
useless ivory box

they rarely track us, even
with their eyes, knowing how
we move through quietude
into their certain regard:
how we will rise from the fog
compliant as tables

WHAT FLOWS

The movement's always downward
of course, from chickens, slimy, small,
small-minded too in common parlance:
the adherence of minutia, clinging
to the soles of our shoes.

Whereas horseshit's larger, sidestepped and
less processed, just piled up, baled almost,
into the daily work we do: just as bullshit
is the easy lie, the grease on the gears,
and later, tall clumps in the field.

But bushshit, that's a lie which doesn't
even trouble to pretend, it's: here's your
ration, eat it and die: we didn't know children
would bleed into the sand, levees would burst,
them darkies float out through the dark.

MAKING LOVE AFTER SURGERY

Easing at it again, careful as scorpions,
except how the loose organs surge in their cave,
everything's surely the same, so I'm surprised
that after months of careful distractions,
just when I might hope some corner's
finally turned, it seems only
my back is and this near-joy slides
down into that muck where blind things
eat each other life after life and love
itself's another bubbled loss – *your side*
or mine she smiles and slips to sleep
while on those shadowed streets I take
even the dogs fall silent as I pass.

WRITING LYN

Past Easter, weeks after your letter asking
if I'd like to go sailing and should you
have children: my morning runs
along the towpath turn to a catalog of May:
shad writhe along the bank, fan eggs
into warm mud while last month's wary mallard
paddle the canal with nine drab young;
in the sycamore, a red patch: grosbeak or warbler:
how can I say no to anything?

The real pleasure of an old story's not
the predicable ending but sharing the premise:
children are the best excuse for ice cream and
baseball; you send on half of yourself and hang onto
random excuses; they weed the vegetables,
give mash to the chickens, add layer after
layer to the topsoil and, unless something terrible happens,
will stand at your grave feeling someone hit their hearts
with sledgehammers:

how could you say no
to anything like that?

STEALING BACK

In early September along the south bank of the river
I found a bush the homeless had missed, a few branches
freighted with blackberries, fat and sweet, and then today,
hurrying off to an appointment uptown, there on the
back corner of a building I'd passed a hundred times
without notice: an arm-thick vine with the shadowed purple
of concord grapes, and though I was running late, I stopped
to try a few and finally took a bunch
                              and the untamed
musk calls back my brother, buried two weeks now:
it is an autumn Saturday midmorning, we're
playing catch, our mother and aunt hanging the wash,
the sheets white as a new ball, cool and damp to slide among
sideways without touching, and after, sneaking into the kitchen
where extra tomatoes bubble on the stove, we scoop them out
by the bowl, sprinkle with sugar as much as we want.

SOLITUDE

I love a woman steeped in solitude
as the narrow canyons where we wind
which deep upon my heart intrude

and truth be told, underscore the mood
even in each other's limbs entwined:
I love a woman steeped in solitude.

Her needs are naked more than nude,
still her hands are on me always kind
and deep upon my heart intrude

like an ancient story of being viewed
by one who smiles and thus unbinds.
I love a woman so steeped in solitude

even absence is now with her imbued
as a winter grace I am consigned
which deep upon my heart intrudes

like a tongue that won't be misconstrued
but licks my blood dumb and blind.
And this so upon my heart intrudes
I love that woman steeped in solitude.

PLANTING FORSYTHIA

Making a bouquet, I think aloud
smiling as though you're here
and me figuring on
still, if it's large enough
perhaps even numbers don't matter but
for a small grouping it needs to be odd –
maybe the eye seeks a center
not in emptiness
but the thing itself,
the particular growth:
root, flower, and seed

WHY I WRITE

A reader came by, she'd
liked a poem and her husband –
she had, she said, "the sweetest husband" –
he'd hired a calligrapher and now
would I sign too?

As if I never wrote in thin hope
some day dreary as another,
some cold wet January maybe
a long and lovely Inge
would slide through time like a trout.

We talked – books we
loved and quantum physics.
She was tall and laughed out loud,
her tongue full of zen,
her eyes sun gold plain.

She read Husserl and Heidegger and
took my silence deep when
as ever faced with
beauty, I'm speechless, I'm
no smarter than that.

DEDICATION

It is tempting to consider the deceptive solidity
of brick and steel, even of glass, tempting to call this
a *building*, twisting the verb to a noun the way endless
occasions of energy are woven into matter. It is tempting
to believe when we see walls and floors, that we behold a
structure, or that we can trace wires and duct work and call it
a *system*, and to think we have named the sacred names.

But that is not how it is. Whatever is good
flows out of emptiness. Whatever sings
reverberates through a void. The work of our souls
is always in spaces between. We live in
Chinese landscapes where the paper is mostly
left untouched, in what some might call negative space,
as if the air were either opposed to us or else nothing.

But if you think air is nothing, ask the night tramps
huddled beneath the railroad bridge. Ask the runaways
trolling West Second, the year scraping toward Christmas,
while we read about Misty, her head crushed with a brick, beaten
past need, or even utility, ripped out of everything except
the seamless past as we slide by in heated cars,
pretending tomorrow we'll really care.

There is a world, maybe, where the quarters are always
shiny, where no one has to choose between food and medicine.
There is a world maybe everyone knows, every day,
our lives are brief flares in the darkness, and it doesn't matter what
we choose slammed against the bricks, cigarettes or blindfolds.
What matters is what happens in the spaces between the walls,
what happens standing daily in the open doorways of our hearts.

by intention ...

ELEMENTAL DESIGNS

TO MY DAUGHTER'S CREDITORS

Taking each day as it rose and still
stripping further, moving toward Ireland
in a wandering minimalist way, she left only
a few books, some clothes, a little music:

no savings accounts, no checking accounts, no
charge cards, no cash in the mattress, no
IRAs nor plans for such. Nor was there
health insurance

except what the State provides. No
life insurance, no disability: a single-car fatality
in a borrowed beat-up minivan
with no coverage in place.

Maybe the State can reimburse
for her last, kind hours;
maybe they still set aside
scraps for the indigent.

Maybe because she gave away
everything,
even her leftover body, the tissue
banks will extend some credit,

but the bottom line remains
there is no estate upon which to lien:
she spent herself like air: breathe in,
breathe out.

CLEANING UP

In the hurricane's steamy afterbreath,
discontent with slower cycles of decay,
mold and mildew, all death's little mouths,
we spark the saws' cicada cries, rake
and heap and thicken the air with smoke
until the sun's red filtered circle hangs
like the solace of holy fire.

Day after day I stand on the edge
of that blaze chosen for my daughter
which gnawed toward a fine gray powder
to be bundled on the mantle, a few
handsfull of dust to scatter on the breeze:
bird cries, the tide easing out.

Wind and rain pass over conserving
again and again energy and matter,
but physics is no consolation,
nor Housman, nor the gods'
many mansions, only the dream

finally to open the door upon a world
blossomed in wholly geometric flames
where even the obsidian teeth in my heart
melt to drops of liquid light.

PERMISSION

my wife sits at the crossword and glances
suddenly up, ambushed by tears
where she's written *tattoo* and
remembered the night nurse whispering

how she's stalled her daughter's request:
just till you're sixteen – and this child
waiting only till you steel yourselves
and sweet lord of mercy, let her go:

that delicate sunburst on her ankle,
the ring feathered upon a finger and
how can we deny them anything when,
her hand falls empty, when this…

and today, she says,
today I'll tell her: now,
go ahead,
do it now

It seems to have skipped me,
that gene which makes rules for music
beyond a sense of inherent joy or
pain, unlike my friend who could explain
so much piano is sad, of course, because
it's in a minor key.

Tonight it's fiddles and pipes and the lilt
of an Edinburgh lady and everyone kicks
their heels in memory's village, oblivious
perhaps to the underlying Celtic melancholy,
leaning back in laughter or laying a head
upon a shoulder.

Or maybe they just dance against it, all the
slipped hopes and bruised good-byes
like old walls working deep into the soil,
and my daughter skipping out among them
over the swirling floor, her meadowlark melody
grace-filled and doomed.

And always I hear that dance we practiced for,
where a young man bows and my girl spins
in perfect balance, love and acceptance,
planting moon, harvest moon, child
after child like waves upon the shore:
that dance we'll never do.

AT THE MORNING MIRROR

ignoring the hair in customary disarray
my eyes assess how the slit skin
puckers around incisions below my
breastbone, above my navel, the promise
wounds will soften over time, and wish
again that lover stretched in early light,
the habitual enchantment of her hands,
how once she murmured: your body, it's just
so perfect, words both generous and relatively
true beside her splendor laced with scars:

that place they pried her children out, living
and dead, the arms that scraped one finally safe
from a well, those splendid skater's legs
on close inspection stitched back to function
and god how I wish her hands inside my shirt,
easing my daughter burned to ash, tracing
where parts of my body, imperfect but
cherished, were excised and thrown away,
and then to stroke with salves or silken craft
and magic, magic, make me whole

ARRANGING THE STONES

On my knees late this Sunday I wrestle
their shapes like eastern states, intertwined
wedges of Virginia and Carolina, night
coming on as mockingbirds sport in the bath
and Icelandic poppies bow shyly to the west.

My sweet neighbor slides through the gate
between her robust hydrangea and my sporadic sage
to ask if I caught the radios crackling when
her morning glance into the river hooked a bag, no,
a body, snagged on trees, just over there.

But I hadn't, with the fan turned against the heat,
and her family refused even to look
as the cops came by boat and dragged
upstream to the flats that black male
she has carried still all day:

how the head turned and the legs
lifted up, questions accidental or violent,
while the southern night fills with the usual fireflies
and what, what will I do now
with Illinois?

CALENDAR

this is the day we last spoke, me rising
to hug as she left, her offhand goodbye

this is the day the phone rang: a crash in the canyon,
the medivac chopper, the rush to critical care

this is the hour we drove in
to hear the neurosurgeons say

the only question is when,
and this is the hour I went to tell our son

this is the day we waited through arrangements
of kin, the kindness of nurses, papers of course

papers to be signed, and scraps of comfort,
her friends taking turns holding her hand,

playing the reggae she loved and maybe
somewhere she heard

this is the day we agreed to let her go and yet
hours and hours and hours and still

she will not relent and the
tortured rasp issues again and again

this is when we are weary beyond asking, when
I sit in the stairwell with my face buried in a towel

making the noise any animal makes
steel on bone

and this is when finally
she just stopped

this is when the color leached out
and the death scent filled the room

this is when we ceased to have
a present tense

this is the night I lay down and there she was
already done with her body,

just five or six spheres of light,
a whirling sleight-of-hand yes

I know you loved me, but of course
I can't say what it's like

this is the day we received food and flowers,
when we paid for the burning and made ourselves busy

this is the night we went to the fireworks
because what else was there to do;

this is the time it was pointless
to be anything except polite

this is the day her friends came with drums and we
blew bubbles and sent off balloons with notes

and everyone cried and said
it was lovely

and this is the day still I wake
with a hole in my heart

this is the day
I will not be consoled

this is always
that day.

OFFERING

I wish I could tell you about the new house,
how close it sits by the river,
how the rooms flow each to each

and where we've put the brass bed your
great grandmother bought used in 1910
and which should have passed to you.

I want to say you could sleep there when you visit,
rattle its bones with your young wrestler,
and maybe stir up some elusive hope.

I want to explain how they're going to cut me again –
there are stones in the bile that drip like Aeschylus,
but it's a minor and necessary loss.

I want to outline the shape of my formal garden
like the ones I recall along the ocean
those summers I was young –

here's foxglove – and those the corners which will
overflow with cosmos, with sweet william
and black-eyed susan,

and here's where you might find me at dusk
laying peat and manure and ashes
at the feet of your yellow rose.

HOLY SATURDAY

I am sick of azaleas, of
dogwood exploding in the undershade,
the buzz of the everyday
fingering earth open again,

sick of the river lolling its bovine tongue
along my ditch, brown, slicked with trash while
the radio repeats mantras of expected crests
from Rocky Mount to Chocowinity,

and I am sick of the octopus
crouched inside my wife,
the tick tick of chemicals
and her patient, gentle surgeon,

sick of mouths and eggs, of hungers
and lures, of dancing and
the parts we offer over and over
if only, if only... and I know

somewhere out on a desert hillside
is the small clearing where my niece wed
her first husband, and my lost angel
still sparkles in that light, and I am

on my knees, Grandfather Piñon,
asking strength, succor, mercy –
it's all much the same
and only time that we have,

the briefest pause in the wind while lichen
conspire into flower and slow as the gods
the rough bark yields up
a single iridescent bubble.

AFTER THE CATARACTS

Late autumn eases into the Carolinas and I submit
to a flurry of tests in the brightness, switch plates sliding
up and down the walls, and am proclaimed healed, eyes
leaking into tissues while the world struggles into focus and

explodes with color – electron wrens at the nucleated thistle,
leaves in all their insistent particularity, the spotted garden
spider's latest temptation draped between the bayberry
and the cannas, clouds backlit by the sun like the dreams
of Benoit Mandelbrot and even the Tar is washed with gold,

and now I am that stranger walking out with my own
daughter's eyes while owls fuss in the sour gum, and
again and again she tugs my sleeve – *this way, this way* –
the whole world as discovery, as treasure – and even
the dying gnats rise like a tongue of sacred fire.

WALKING TODAY

Cottonwood drifts up the stones
along the spring-blatant honeysuckle,
roses bent down with flower:
the river full and dark
where a blunt needle of cormorant rises,
juggles silversided up and into
and floats away, her eyes
snake-proud
while the cool weight of trout
settles into a notion like
immortal soul
or that even the dead,
time to time, can grow

ALMOST HERE

The first day of fall, Cariboo and I take the cool early
above the city's current, the air full with rabbit and quail,
and when she slides through the common's long plush:
each step a shiver of maybe and if:

her lope and slide through the sage, chamisa's
slow and golden swells, our first dreams of flight,
ditch-side willows slipping yellow across
their salmon skin

while I launch milkweed seeds out over
the arroyo, parachuting jungles:
the empty boat-pod perfect
hand and eye

ASHES

In that last fall we split wood,
tamarack and red cedar
which had wintered over twice,

she handling the wedge,
choosing angles of attack
for me to hammer home –

half a cord stacked on the porch
where we took the late sun watching
flickers and sparrows and young cats,

thinking: binocularity –
it's what we like in animals,
that we see related worlds,

distrusting the skink's independent eyes
till the moon risen golden over her shoulder
slid west and silver up the sky.

•

Eventually everything stops:
chemicals, radiation, hope:
even the tumors stop
snaking her brain,
constricting her lungs

and the fire that fuels her breath,
the fire into which we slide
her cold body
even these are still
and we bank against the night.

•

I take them down
my daughter in her wooden box,
my wife in her ceramic cylinder,
empty them into bowls
on the maple table
and fill first the vase
scooping Kirsten, then Jeanne,
four measures each
for me,
then two apiece
for the trip,
and the rest in the box
for when my son visits
early next year

(there are bits of bone
and dust so fine I breathe it in)

my daughter and my wife
who never
are going swimming off Hawaii

•

waves,
shadows:
the moon tips like a gourd
and all the wet stars
pour out upon the sand

SOME OF THIS IS TRUE

My father died last night,
an alcoholic chain-smoking carpenter
with forearms like Popeye and the heart of Jesus Christ:

he was older than a century and
my brother was visiting along with his dead wife
and we were watching my young wife mow the side yard,

our little girl careening about the lawn
falling over and over to marvel at airplanes and
a remnant of the moon –

an agreeable morning, all told:
juice and coffee on the patio,
the late summer lavender bent down with finches,

hummingbird wars more justifiable than our own,
and we could note where the maple have prospered,
how sycamore sprawls and hawthorn clusters

while the talk glided around my dead wife, my dead daughter
laughing at liquid time as the trees work
both up and down, arching and anchoring,

though people just drift in from the sky, seed and
burrow root over root until we are lost even
to our children's dreams.

But only some of this true.

COLOPHON

Designed and produced at the Black Rock Press by Bob Blesse.
The typeface is Minion, designed by Robert Slimbach.
Printed by BookMobile, Minneapolis, Minnesota.
Thanks to Steve Lautermilch for his cover image.

BLACK ROCK PRESS